The Art of Magickal
Enchantment

Influence, Command and Control

a practical grimoire from
The Order of Unveiled Faces

Theodore Rose

Contents

The Triangle of Fortune

Five years ago, only months after I had completed the first grimoire, my publisher asked me to produce another book, such had been the popularity of the original. My resistance arose immediately as I had no desire to cheapen the primary work by producing an unwanted sequel.

The writing was not an issue, as most of my work has already been supplied in summary form to members of my order. My concern is that magick books have become more like snack food. They are consumed and discarded. If I am going to share magick, I have no wish for it to be discussed, analysed, and studied, for it is only through the use of magick that you can come to know its power.

My refusal was not an act of stubbornness, but a lingering doubt about the quality of the readership. I have been informed, and shown evidence of, a great success that is widespread among readers of my first work. With this truth and five years, I am now permitted by my own conscience and the laws I choose to uphold, to reveal further work.

A reasonable and accurate understanding is that the first book was well-liked because I took the time to right wrongs, correct errors, and dispel the myths being spread by a malodorous couple of psychotic pretenders who were flogging their filthy oils and herbs while writing a child-like collection of spoofed spells and rituals that had no bearing on the reality of magick. While I was also pleased to do anything to crush such pretenders, that was a side-effect that was never sought. It was, however, enjoyed.

The purpose of our time together here is not to entertain by bringing others down or by sharing works of greatness. It may appear to outsiders that with a collection of fierce magick to my name, that implies I am a stone-faced occultist creating misery so that I can benefit. This inference is false, as will be shown in the present work. There is far more benefit to be found in cooperation than you may consider, and the most polished enchantment retains cooperation as an essence of its power.

You may be disappointed to know that enchantment involves cooperation, with benefits being passed to the one you enchant. I encourage you to resist such disappointment, as when you look beyond the most obvious facts as they are presented, there are many ways to alter and revise these rituals to create results that are not obviously so cooperative. This is to say that although each ritual will be framed to help both you and the one you enchant, it can be crafted in ways that enable you to control and manipulate.

Enchantment has different meanings influenced by the context in which it is used, but in general, it is known to refer to the act of casting a spell or using altered or supernatural powers to influence or manipulate someone or something. What I present to you in this book is a method for using magick to affect another person (or a group of people) in a way that benefits you. And while enchantment can influence others to perform actions that are not in their best interest, it is not a force of psychopathic cruelty. Let us not forget that in a broader sense, enchantment can also refer to a feeling of delight, wonder, or fascination, as if one is under a magickal or mystical spell. We often say we are enchanted by the most prosaic of wonders.

You are not, therefore, being given a manual for turning others into enslaved zombies or submissive victims. This is not a handbook of magickal instruction for those who wish to seduce aggressively, deceive for pleasure, or mislead the unwary for the joy of making them suffer. Nor is it for those wishing to engage in curse rituals or magickal attacks. Should you require that brand of magick, you are advised to explore *Lucifer and The Hidden Demons*. With enchantment magick, you work neither with demons nor angels or other analogous spirits. The elemental forces in this book are known as salamanders or fire spirits.

Greatly misunderstood, the magick of salamanders requires you to look for an outcome (or result as it is often known) that benefits both you and the one you enchant. This requires some shrewd work on your part, but nothing that is beyond your ability. Discerning the correct way to frame your magickal desire guides and structures your magickal intent and is the fundamental aspect of these workings that safeguards success.

It is true that elemental magick can be used to cause such harm, but my advice is to understand that the subtle art of enchantment is one that requires you to think more deeply than usual. You are required to find a solution that benefits you and the one being enchanted, and this does not have to diminish the benefit you receive. You can get exactly what you desire, and by benefitting another, you create magick that is incapable of harming you.

Without any doubt, you are protected while engaging with these powers, but you do not have permission to use this magick to attempt works of 'darkness' that are meant only to harm others. Even if such permission were granted by myself, or any other instructor of occult methodology, it would be a false permission, tempting you into a rash act. If you long for a book of curses or any surly form of mind manipulation, you know where to seek such magick. Those powers cannot be found here. This does not mean, however, that's enchantment is weak or undermines your ability to get what you want. Should you decide that an annoying person who lives near to your home must be removed, you could curse, make weak, and otherwise deflate that person's will, but you may never get compliance. To influence, you enchant. And in sending that person away, you give them the gift of starting over in a location where they will be welcome.

Providing you with more examples, to illustrate the surgical precision you can achieve with such fiery magick, assume your enemy is consumed with hatred for you. This is unsettling for you both, for to hate may be more draining than to be the one who is hated. You can choose to end the hatred of your enemy, and in doing so, you both benefit.

This is not a moral code, but a code of practice developed after many years of exploring the true potential of the fire spirits. Amongst the most misunderstood, falsely maligned, and corrupted spirits to appear on the fringe of occultism, the fire spirits shall be revealed to you, with their powers and the method for contacting them to create the situations you demand.

Enchantment is more powerful than ordinary magick as it creates a triangle of fortune. The three points of this triangle are you, the act of magick, and the other person. Each point is intimately connected to the other two, affecting them while being affected by them. The magick you produce is symbiotic in nature, and cooperation with the target is both covert and essential. You are not setting out to destroy an enemy but to destroy a situation that displeases you. When enchanting another, you do not overpower them for the pleasure of seeing them submit but to share in the benefits of a changed situation.

Those people who feel magick should be dark and vicious are using magick as a costume when it should be a practice that brings your will to bear.

You may have become aware that throughout its relatively modern history (during the last two hundred years), occultism has been plagued by pamphlets. Rapidly written booklets, too short to matter and filled with insufficient content. That was my view for many a long year. It then came to my attention that some of those minor pamphlets did excellent work in constraining the complexities of magick and making occultism palatable. No longer the perverse cash cows I perceived them to be, these pamphlets, short books, or even essays were the mainstay of practical occultism. My concern remained that such books might trivialise the occult into a short spell book, making the users of its technology believe it is no more than a mild self-help technique. When you accept that the supreme procedures of magick can be shared in short books, you are freed from insisting that all magick books be long and complex.

In the past five years I have heard occultists bemoan the growth of occult publishing, with many fakes abounding. I agree that books written at speed by poorly educated newcomers, and filled with promises (to hide the author's ignorance) are a stain on occultism. This should not, however, prejudice us against works that are succinct. There are far too many long books being published that are packed with hundreds of ineffective spirits and threadbare methods for making contact.

The irony presented here is that this book is short, almost a pamphlet. Could a small book really change your life? I believe that the greatest magickal truths could be written on the back of an envelope. There is no need to be overly expressive. This is more than an excuse for creating a short book but is an encouragement. You are encouraged to realise that magick does not have to be a long-winded affair and that a short book with precise instructions may be all you require. I will, therefore, get to the matter in hand and cover the workings and effects of this most practical magick.

The Knowledge of Fire

The history of the spirits in this book may be of little interest to you, and I share the story to illustrate several salient points and to enable an understanding of why this magick can work for you. The knowledge can help to remove the barriers of doubt, which cloud the magickal effect.

History is a word that equates to boredom for those who found history lessons tiresome, so let us say instead that we are exploring the story of the salamanders, the spirits of fire, and the secret origins of this magick.

The most well-known sources for the magick are two magick pamphlets that were not only short but largely fictional.

The Black Pullet, first published in the late 18th century, is attributed to an anonymous French officer who allegedly served in Napoleon's army and claimed to have discovered the book during his travels in Egypt. Rescued by a mysterious man, he is taken away and fed with secrets. This tale may sound exciting but discard it as fiction. This fictional device was used to deliver the content of the pamphlet, being nothing other than a framework for disseminating the concepts.

A short text, *The Black Pullet* consists of only a few dozen pages, and it primarily focuses on the creation and use of talismans and amulets for practical effect, although the purposes listed are inaccurate and ineffective.

One of the most distinctive features of *The Black Pullet* is its use of a 'magical hen' or 'black pullet' that is said to have the power to grant wishes and answer questions. According to the most literal interpretation, the hen is supposed to lay golden eggs. As a serious occultist, you surely recognize this as a metaphor rather than an attempt to breed poultry with magickal powers.

The pamphlet provides instructions for obtaining and caring for the hen, as well as rituals for using its magick. Another irony is that this part of the book contains no magick at all and is only a symbolic representation of the magickal act itself and guidance on how it should be performed.

Looking beyond its relatively obscure status and questionable origins, one can see that *The Black Pullet* has remained a popular and influential text in the occult community. It continues to be studied and used by some modern sorcerers and occultists. I am one of those, although I can say with a high degree of confidence that the only content worth retaining is found in the Words of Power used to summon the salamanders. Although it is stated that these are not words, but names, they have a dual purpose. While being the names for calling the fire spirits, they are also Words of Power that call on the *qualities* of *many* connected salamanders to work for you at one time on a coordinated quest.

Another book, more difficult to obtain until recent years, is *The Black Screech Owl*, also known as *The Treasure of the Old Man of the Pyramids*. The text is by no means identical to *The Black Pullet*, but its essence is familiar, and the same Words of Power are found.

The sigils are drawn in a more ornate manner, leading one to suspect they are an elaboration on what had gone before. Given that the sigils in *The Black Pullet* are an ugly mixture of proto-Hebrew, Arabic, Celestial Letters, and alchemical symbols, along with undeniably bad drawing, they lack the power to achieve anything at all. The sigils in *The Black Screech Owl* have done away with much of this finery, but also contain random elements, such as inappropriate sigils lifted from other grimoires. As a standalone text, it is almost worthless, but the Words of Power, repeated here, will hold our interest.

The work of an originator (that is, one who invents modern magick), is to discern what has gone before and build on it for the betterment of occult expression. While originators can invent entirely new concepts, that is not their only purpose. As originators, in The Order of Unveiled Faces, we do not believe that magick stopped being formed a few hundred years ago. You may laugh, and yet how many times have occultists reassured you that you are being sold good magick because it is so old, ancient, and authentic?

Let us never forget that if humans once had the ability to connect with spirits and create great grimoires and ritual methods, we are capable of doing the same now.

With wider knowledge and better means of communication, we are more providentially placed to create new magick. You should not be aghast if I were to invent a completely new magickal system and present it to you without any glance back at previously discovered methods or spirits. Perhaps I will do so, to prove the point.

For now, let us agree that we believe it is a fallacy to suggest that the only good magickal knowledge is old magickal knowledge. The impression of being old and therefore authoritative is nonsense, as can be illustrated by these blackbird pamphlets, which have no practical outlet.

As originators, we do not ignore the past, and where we can, we explore what has gone before with more forceful precision than is generally seen. It is essential to discover every aspect of a working that can be applied to a modern method.

Using this approach, there was yet another irony, in that in attempting to create modern magick from the Words of Power, we were led to older sources containing the same words, again affirming (as is generally accepted) that the Words of Power call on the specific energies of the fire spirits.

The fiery salamanders are a source of extremely powerful magick, but the method we created is not entirely new. Originators, as I have said, can invent magick, but they can also combine forms of magick that have worked before, to make something new. That is what you find in this book. It is not a rehash of *The Black Pullet* or an elaboration of *The Black Screech Owl*. While they offered clues as to the names that might be used, and methods that should be contrived, those books can otherwise be dismissed.

Elemental magick has its uses but is less popular than other forms of ritual practice. This may be because the spirits are somewhat opaque to the practitioner. It may also be because too many books have summarised dogma and tried to package it as a breakthrough.

Should your desire be to know and understand salamanders, I hope you feel compelled to try the magick shared in these pages. When you obtain a result through the means of elemental magick, you will have a strong and intuitive sense of what the fire spirits are to you.

Were you to ask me how to describe the true nature of an angel, demon, or even a human, or for that matter, a snail, I could not do so to the satisfaction most would demand. With spirits of all kinds, experience always wins over fancy descriptions and conceptually moulded realities. That is, you will learn about the fire spirits by working with them.

I can say that the spirits have a form of consciousness and compassion for those who call for their aid. You may sense energy or personality associated with each spirit. You may never sense them directly at all. You will, however, be safe, as their names bring protection and cooperation the moment they are spoken.

You understand now that the fire spirits can be called through a combination of sigils and Words of Power. The method is extraordinarily plain and requires you only to think about your two desires while looking at the sigil and speaking words.

You may have noticed that I spoke of two desires. Each ritual requires a desire for yourself and a desire for the one being enchanted.

The sigils are not essential for contact but were developed to make contact with the fire spirits easier and to ensure that the translation of your thoughts and feelings is clear. Our sigils were drawn, and redrawn, over the last thirty years, based on our evocations of the conscious bodies that arise briefly from the fire spirits. Put succinctly, one could say we threw away the sigils that didn't work and refined those that did. I am pleased to share these unique sigils with you in this book. They are the focus of this work, connecting your thoughts to the Words of

Power, and embedding those within the spirits, who work on your desires to make them become real.

Let us then, move on to the technique itself, and keep this book short enough that it may be called a pamphlet, and in no way shall we let that denigrate the potential of what we learn here.

The Ritual

The ritual should be performed in private, in a place where you can bring calm focus to your work. Silence is optional, but you should not work where other people are making noise, or with music or entertainment disturbing the atmosphere. The requirement is to bring your attention to the ritual and keep it there for the duration.

Any time of day or night is acceptable, and other considerations, such as astrological correspondences, are irrelevant. Perform no more than one ritual on any day, and resist performing lightweight rituals with great frequency. Instead, focus on rituals that feel as though they might bring a significant and worthwhile benefit.

The magick is more potent when your desire is strong. When this magick is reserved for times of more distinct and specific need, it works directly. You will not benefit from using this magick for minor matters, but when a concern is of importance to you, when you feel the need, this magick can bypass your doubts and insecurities, and even the crippling desires that ruin many magickal attempts. This does not mean every situation must be life or death for you to enchant, but you should not enchant for the sake of a trivial change or minor entertainment. Change should come because you genuinely desire that change.

Follow the instructions precisely but without concern for being so precise that you become nervous or paranoid about your methodology. Do this, and all will follow as it should.

Your request will be formulated, not necessarily as a spoken sentence, but as an impression, a mental summary of your desire. You will use your imagination, and no matter how limited your imagination may appear to be from your vantage point, you are assured that it will be sufficient to enable the required contact and express your desires. Imagination is not necessarily an act of creating strong and realistic images. Imagination is no different to thinking about what you want, and that is something we spend a great deal of time doing. This should be effortless. All you need to do is think about what you want, in whatever form is comfortable for you. That may be in words, images, sentences, feelings, or a rush of emotions and sensations.

Should you find that you can only think about your desires in a simple way, without feelings or images, you are still giving the magick the information it needs to engage the elemental spirits to work for you.

Think of your desires as a request. You have two desires that are intermingled. One benefits you directly, and one desire benefits the person that you enchant. Think about this before the ritual and think about what the result will mean to you.

While I will admit that this requirement may be too demanding on those infirm of mind or uncertain of desire, it should be a small challenge indeed. You are only required to use your cunning to get what you want and find a way to benefit the other party. I have already stated, with sufficient clarity, that this does not mean you are negating your result but strengthening it through directing your results carefully.

In each of the pages that describe the powers available to you, brief examples will give you some insight into how the power might be used. These examples are the merest of starting points and should be used for reference, before designing the powers you wish to apply to your situation.

The first of the powers (to make somebody adore you) goes into this in slightly more detail and should help establish a pattern for using the rest of the book.

It's important to ensure clarity when forming a request to these spirits but avoid placing any restrictions on how the desired outcome should manifest. If your intention is to use enchantment to extract the truth from someone, it's wise not to limit the potential of the magick by selecting a particular time, place, method, or situation for this to occur. While your desire should be clear, it shouldn't be limited in scope. A vague desire is less potent than a precise one, but imposing explicit precision can become a limitation. Therefore, only impose as much precision as is necessary to bring you satisfaction, neither more nor less.

To initiate the ritual, no preliminary invocation, call, gesture, or other symbolic action is necessary because there will be no doubt in your mind as to what is happening. Since you are aware that you are summoning a fire spirit, there is no need for any ceremony, calls to ancient gods, permission from angels, or declarations of intent.

You don't need to know the spirits physical appearance, or even have a sense of its nature. The act of making the intention to perform magick is one of the most powerful aspects of *any* magick, and the intention to perform magick brings about the required connection to the spirits.

For each of the following powers, you will find instructions regarding their nature and the way you can craft desires and requests to match their abilities and specialities. On the page after this, you will see the sigil that commands the presence of the required fire spirit. At the bottom of that page are the Words of Power that you will speak during the ritual. A short phonetic guide follows beneath that so that everything you need is visible on a single page.

The ritual commences with you speaking all the words of power, once each. Should you have studied *The Black Pullet*, or other similar sources, you will note that some words are for summoning, others for restricting or guiding powers, and some to dismiss the spirits. Such formulations were either a blind to fool the uneducated or a mistake made by those who did not understand the cooperative nature of the spirits. Forget any previous knowledge and treat the 'names' as Words of Power to summon the spirits and guide their power.

You may also note that the spellings used here are not all identical to those in the more popular renderings of *The Black Pullet*. While exact spelling is never as important as it may seem, this book contains only the spellings that our Order has found to be effective. Do not be alarmed if they don't match with something more familiar to you. The same applies to pronunciation. What I have given you is sufficient, even if your own language is not English. Pronunciation gets less and less important the more context a word is given. The context of combined spirit power is implied by each name and its connection to the others. This safeguards against any difficulty with pronunciation.

As stated, you speak all the Words of Power. When they have all been spoken, let your gaze rest on the sigil. You do not study the sigil but keep it within view as you consider the two results you want. Spend a few moments at least, but up to a minute or more if you wish, considering the result you want. Feel emotions if you feel them. See images if you see them.

Your eyes can rest on the sigil or move them over it. You can blink, and you do not need to stare but remain aware of the sigil.

If there is nothing but words or ideas in your mind, that is also thinking, and that is as it should be. You cannot make a mistake here. When you feel you have been clear in stating your request, by thinking about it for a short time (and no more than five minutes), speak the Words of Power once more.

You will occasionally feel something change at this moment like a psychological switch being flicked. This sensation can be electrical or may even produce flickers of light. You may feel a small thud on your skin, anywhere on your body. You may feel nothing, and all is well; whatever you feel, your ritual has concluded.

This is about as simple as magick can be, but do not let the simplicity fool you into considering it to be trivial.

Once the ritual has concluded, give it no more mind. If you can work toward your goal through your own actions, magick connects to your effort and streamlines its intelligence to match yours.

If there is nothing you can do to further your cause, as may be the case, avoid dwelling on your need for the result. Instead, assume that the result will come.

Some rituals fail. In almost all cases, rituals fail because the one casting a spell or performing a ritual does so with too large a demand, or with too great a sense of impatience and urgency.

Never let the enchanted person know what you are doing. Whether they are enemies or friends, you should keep your work secret from them. Exposing your magick to them, at any time, can nullify its effects. You may tell others, and celebrating magick is often beneficial, but never speak of this work to the one you enchanted, unless it's your intention to negate the original effects.

The remainder of this book goes over the individual powers while providing the required Words of Power, and the sigils, and a brief pronunciation guide. You have all you need to enchant others, and while you should be in no hurry, I believe you will see results faster than expected.

Finding Enchantment

Having selected a problem or situation that requires your magickal influence, you will choose an appropriate enchantment. The following groupings may be a key to finding the power you need, although you will need to read the whole book to gain a complete understanding of each power.

Interpersonal Influence
Enchant a person to adore your company   29
Enchant a person to respect you   65
Enchant a person to give you valuable guidance   105
Enchant a group to follow you like a leader   41
Enchant a group to welcome your ideas   69
Enchant a person to be open-minded   73
Enchant a person to trust you with money   97

Conflict Resolution
Enchant a group to overcome a common obstacle   61
Enchant a person to stop legal action against you   89
Enchant your enemies to reveal their plans   57
Enchant your enemies to become silent with fear   53
Enchant your enemies to see your point of view

Memory and Information Manipulation
Enchant a person to forget a painful memory   33
Enchant a person to keep your secrets   49
Enchant your enemies to reveal their plans   57

Emotional Influence
Enchant a person to adore your company   29
Enchant your enemies to become silent with fear   53

Offense Magick

Truth and Transparency

Money

Emotional Healing

Leadership and Influence

Personal Growth

Tactical Advantage

Subterfuge

Dominance over Enemies

Enchant a person to adore your company

By harnessing this power, you, as the enchanter, can inspire strong affection in another person, making them eager for your presence. This enchantment can be employed to enhance relationships, cultivate loyalty, or simply make your interactions more enjoyable and rewarding.

This power can significantly enhance the quality of your interactions with the other party, making your time spent together more enjoyable and fulfilling. This can lead to improved emotional well-being and a more vibrant social life.

A person who adores your company is likely to be more supportive, loyal, and helpful towards you. They may go out of their way to assist you, offering their resources or skills when you need them. This can lead to practical advantages in various aspects of your life, from personal tasks to professional projects.

The ability to make someone adore your company will ensure you can command respect from others and enhance your reputation, further solidifying your social standing.

To devise a benefit for the target of your magick, you can frame this around your ego, believing that people will be better off for knowing you. If you cannot believe this, assume that having them adore your company is far better than having them feel uncomfortable around you.

There are additional ways to frame this. You may assume that the enjoyment of your presence can contribute to their overall happiness and satisfaction. It's always a pleasure to be in the company of someone you truly appreciate.

Their affection for you may lead to them having more positive social experiences, fostering a sense of belonging and connection. This can contribute significantly to their social well-being.

Their relationship with you could offer them opportunities to learn, grow, and have enriching experiences. They may gain from your wisdom, experience life from a new perspective, or be exposed to new ideas and possibilities through their association with you.

You can see that the framing of this magick requires a small degree of double-think. You may have no genuine desire to bring benefits to the person you enchant, but you can *frame* the situation in a way that makes it *seem* like they will benefit. This is all that's required for the fire spirits to respond. Going forward through this book, you will see you can achieve almost anything you desire by twisting things to *seem* as though they benefit the other party.

The enchantment to make a person adore your company is a powerful tool for enhancing social connections and interactions. Its strength lies in its ability to foster affection and loyalty, offering benefits to both you, the enchanter, and the individual who finds delight in your presence.

In essence, this enchantment is about cultivating affection and enriching social experiences. It's an enchantment that promotes positive interactions, mutual growth, and a sense of belonging, while also enabling you to control the affections of another when that suits your needs.

Siras, Etar, Besanar

Siras: SEE-ras
Etar: EE-tar
Besanar: beh-SAH-nar

Enchant a person to forget a painful memory

When you are close to somebody who has suffered from trauma, you feel the force of all that fallout. You may also want to heal somebody, out of compassion. This enchantment serves as a potential remedy for trauma, fostering healing, and promoting overall mental wellbeing.

The power also has protective value. When you spend your life with somebody who stores unfortunate memories about you, there are benefits to having those memories fade away.

Does the memory have to be a painful one? You can use this power to make somebody forget anything you like, but it is far more effective with memories that cause pain to the individual in question.

Unlike many powers, the benefit to the other person here is obvious, but we should look in more detail at how this could benefit you.

By facilitating the forgetting of a painful memory, you can bring about a significant transformation in a person's life. Removing such a memory can alter their perspective, emotions, and behaviour, effectively reshaping their personal narrative. This reshaping power can serve to strengthen *your* relationship if you choose that to be the case. A less dignified way of saying this is that if you are tired of somebody's trauma and pain, you will find relief.

The act of erasing a painful memory can lead to improved relations with the person you help. They may view you as a saviour or benefactor, potentially enhancing your bond with them. This strengthened relationship can yield numerous social and emotional benefits for you.

It should be noted that demonstrating the ability to remove a painful memory commands respect and awe from the people you heal, even though they will not be consciously aware of your power.

For the individual who forgets a painful memory, this enchantment offers profound benefits. The removal of a painful memory can significantly alleviate their mental distress, potentially promoting overall happiness. They get a chance to move on, unburdened by the weight of past traumas.

Forgetting a painful memory can lead to new beginnings. Freed from the constraints of the past, they can approach their future with a fresh perspective, opening up new possibilities for growth and exploration.

The enchantment to make a person forget a painful memory is a powerful tool for promoting healing and new beginnings. It can reshape personal narratives, offering benefits to both you, the enchanter, and the individual freed from the chains of a painful memory.

In essence, this enchantment is about healing and transformation, but there is no harm at all in twisting this to your advantage.

Nades, Suradis, Maniner, Sader, Prostas, Solaster

Nades: NAH-des
Suradis: soo-RAH-dees
Maniner: MAH-nin-err
Sader: SAH-der
Prostas: PROS-tas
Solaster: soh-LAS-ter

Enchant a person to realise they have been deceived

By wielding this power, you enlighten an individual to the deception they have been subjected to, or to deception that is currently underway. This enchantment can be an invaluable asset in breaking the chains of manipulation, fostering clarity, and promoting informed decision-making.

If you are certain that a person has been deceived, the benefits are clear. If you are less certain or *suspect* harmful deception, perform the ritual regardless and allow it to work if deception is truly at hand.

Enabling someone to realise they are a victim of deception can offer several advantages. It allows you to reveal the true nature of third parties, potentially safeguarding the enchanted person from further harm or manipulation. This can establish you as a protector and a reliable ally.

By breaking the veil of deceit, you can sway the balance of influence. If the deception was benefiting a rival or adversary, revealing it can undermine their position and elevate yours. This can lead to a shift in alliances and power dynamics.

In the simplest terms, this power can solve a problem. When you know the deception is causing problems for you, use the ritual to reveal the truth and the problem will be solved. Family arguments over wills come to mind.

For the person who has been deceived, this enchantment can lead to transformative benefits. Firstly, in the most obvious terms, understanding the deception can free them from manipulation, enabling them to regain their autonomy. This newfound freedom can be a liberating experience.

The realisation can serve as a valuable lesson, making them more vigilant and sceptical in the future. This can help them guard against future deceptions, equipping them with an essential life skill.

This revelation can lead to introspection and self-improvement. The understanding of how they were deceived can guide them in recognising their vulnerabilities and working on them. This self-improvement journey can lead to personal growth and resilience.

The enchantment to make a person realise they have been deceived is a potent tool for breaking manipulative controls and promoting enlightenment. It offers benefits to both you, the enchanter, and the person who is freed from the shackles of deceit.

In essence, this enchantment is about unveiling the truth and promoting personal autonomy. It's an enchantment that fosters growth and resilience, enabling individuals to navigate their lives with greater clarity and wisdom. And for you, the possibilities of this power will become more apparent the more often you use it for something that matters.

Onaim, Perantes, Rasonastos

Onaim: oh-NAYM
Perantes: peh-RAN-tees
Rasonastos: rah-soh-NAH-stos

Enchant a group to follow you like a leader

This power is directed at a group of people. You may wonder if it can be used on just one or two people, and while it can, its strength is most potent when there is a group of five or more people. It will even work on large groups that remain unknown to you in person.

Be certain that being followed is what you want, and know that your actions must then convey leadership, or those who follow you will soon tire of your inaction.

With this power, you can mobilize a collective effort towards achieving shared objectives or advocating for shared interests. This collective power can amplify your influence and impact in ways that single-handed efforts often cannot.

In addition, the support of a group can bolster your reputation and stature. With people standing by your side, it adds to your credibility and augments your authority. This can help you gain more influence, command respect, and navigate socio-political landscapes more effectively.

Leading a group can offer you a rich learning experience. It can help you hone your leadership skills, understand group dynamics, and foster your ability to inspire and motivate. This can be an enriching experience, or it can be one that gives you more ability to control and manipulate.

The benefit to the group you enchant is less obvious, but I frame it to suggest that following me gives that group a safe place, a home, and a direction. Put bluntly, having a leader to follow makes people feel safe, secure, and even confident. Depending on the personality of the people you enchant, being led by you may bring them great comfort.

Should the group you enchant contain a highly individualistic person, who rarely follows or admires anyone, you will still get results (as they will be compelled to follow the group), but you may expect less loyalty from such people. When this occurs, single out the individual (if known to you in person) and enchant them to admire you. The combination is extremely effective but note that it is only required when resistant individuals in a group are encountered. This can occur in a business setting, for example.

In the absence of leadership, groups often flounder; your guidance can offer them a path to follow and goals to strive for.

Under your leadership, the group members can learn and grow. They can observe your methods, absorb your values, and learn from your experiences. This can lead to their personal and professional development.

Being part of a group following a leader can foster a sense of community and camaraderie among the members. This shared allegiance can create strong bonds, which can contribute to their social wellbeing and collective resilience.

The strength of this magickal tool lies in fostering unity and purpose, although how this unity is used is down to your discretion.

Nitrae, Radou, Sunandam

Nitrae: NEE-tray
Radou: rah-DOO
Sunandam: soo-NAN-dam

Enchant a person to tell you the truth

Secrets can be a source of power or a miasma of pettiness, which means that for the enchanter, uncovering a secret can be a life-changing moment. The power of this enchantment is to make people close to you tell the truth, in a loose-tongued manner that can even cause them to reveal deep secrets or make confessions.

By invoking this enchantment, you can inspire individuals to shed the cloak of falsehood and share their authentic thoughts, emotions, and experiences even when they have previously been highly secretive.

When others are compelled to tell you the truth, you gain the capacity to make informed decisions, foster genuine connections, and build relationships based on trust and authenticity.

The enchantment can be pivotal in situations where clarity is needed, misinformation is rampant, or the stakes are high. Knowing the truth can give you a significant advantage. It allows you to make well-informed decisions, enabling you to navigate your life or strategies more effectively. When others may be misled by deceptions, your enchantment ensures you stay enlightened.

The truth can be an effective tool for uncovering deception or duplicity. If you suspect someone of dishonesty, expose their lies with this magick, protecting you from potential harm or betrayal.

In the most basic of situations, you may be tired of a liar keeping secrets, and this magick will enable you to compel them to spill the truth with the smallest amount of pressure. Sometimes, no pressure at all is required.

To devise benefits for the enchanted individual, frame it as a pathway to self-discovery, growth, and liberation. By embracing truth-telling, they can break free from the burden of dishonesty, cultivate self-awareness, and nurture deeper connections with others. Encourage them to embrace vulnerability, recognizing the transformative power of honesty.

Liberated from the shackles of deception, they may experience a sense of relief, personal growth, and the opportunity to cultivate a more meaningful and honest relationship with you. The power can relieve them of the burden of maintaining lies or deceptions. For many, the act of truth-telling can be liberating, reducing stress associated with maintaining false pretences.

Telling the truth encourages authenticity and fosters personal integrity. These traits are universally appreciated and can enhance personal and professional relationships.

Being compelled to tell the truth can lead to more honest and open communication. It can help them establish a pattern of sincerity, which could prove beneficial in their future interactions.

In many cases, lies are a burden, and this magick works by making the person you enchant believe that the truth with set them free and bring relief. Whether it does or not is up to you and what you do in response.

Noctar, Raiban, Biranther, Nocdar

Noctar: NOHK-tar
Raiban: RYE-bahn
Biranther: bee-RAN-ther
Nocdar: NOHK-dar

Enchant a person to keep your secrets

Inspire unwavering trust and a steadfast commitment in others to guard your confidence. This power not only shields your private truths from being exposed but fosters a bond of loyalty, trust, and mutual respect.

The advantages of this power are legion, but the most apparent is that the enchantment provides you with a profound sense of security, when you fear that another may reveal all that they know. This ritual will bind them into silence and can play a crucial role in maintaining privacy and ensuring the sanctity of your hidden truths.

When a person is enchanted to keep your secrets, you gain the benefit of having a confidant. You can share your thoughts, plans, or experiences without the fear of them being revealed. This offers a safe outlet for your emotions and ideas, which can have therapeutic benefits and aid in stress relief.

Additionally, trust in someone's ability to keep your secrets can deepen your relationship with them, fostering a stronger bond of trust. This shared secrecy can lead to a unique, intimate connection, strengthening your interpersonal relationships.

In some cases, sharing the information may be liberating. You are released from the burden of carrying confidential information alone. With someone else safeguarding your secrets, you can experience a newfound peace of mind, allowing you to focus on other aspects of your life with greater clarity and freedom.

Where there is little or no trust, and somebody has information they can use against you, the magick can work more like a binding, sealing the secrets away and bringing you protection.

For the enchanted person, there are benefits to be gained as well. Being entrusted with your secrets boosts their self-esteem and sense of importance. It conveys a profound trust in their integrity, fostering a deepened sense of self-worth and honour. It also offers them the opportunity to cultivate their own reputation as reliable and trustworthy individuals.

Being privy to your secrets can give them a broader perspective on your life, thoughts, or strategies. This insight can enrich their understanding, potentially influencing their own perspectives or decisions.

The act of keeping secrets can train them in discretion and trustworthiness. These qualities are valued in many personal and professional environments, enhancing their reputation and interpersonal skills.

If the person has secrets they could use against you, the benefit for them could be one of safety. The magick will make them know, on an extremely deep level, that crossing you is a risk. They will be safer if they keep your secrets.

This enchantment safeguards secrets while nurturing a unique bond between two individuals, that, one way or another, will keep your secrets safe.

Zorami, Zaitux, Elastot

Zorami: zoh-RAH-mee
Zaitux: ZAY-tuks
Elastot: ee-LAS-tot

Enchant your enemies to become silent with fear

Embark on a journey into the depths of this formidable power, designed to instil silence and trepidation within your adversaries. By invoking this enchantment, you can command a sense of fear that renders your enemies powerless and immobilized, creating a shield of protection and empowering yourself in challenging circumstances.

The power holds great potential for self-preservation and defence. It grants you the ability to silence those who seek to harm or undermine you, neutralizing their capacity to act against your interests. Its power serves as a deterrent, sending a clear message that any attempts to oppose or confront you will be met with overwhelming intimidation.

By wielding this power, you, as the enchanter, can instil such a potent fear in your adversaries that they are left speechless. This enchantment can alter the dynamics of opposition, giving you a considerable advantage in any conflict, whether open and direct or covert.

Silencing your enemies can provide you with significant control over the narrative. Without opposition, your voice becomes the dominant one, allowing you to sway opinions, control information flow, and assert your authority more readily.

A silent enemy is less likely to act against you. Paralysed by fear, their plans or offensive strategies can be significantly hampered. This can create space for you to manoeuvre, seize opportunities, or even neutralize the threat they pose.

Instilling fear in your enemies can bolster your image of power and might. This perception can discourage potential adversaries, creating a protective aura around you. It reinforces your position and validates your enchanting abilities, enhancing your confidence and reputation.

For your enemies, this fear-induced silence, while seemingly detrimental, can offer unexpected benefits. Firstly, it may force them to confront their fears, pushing them to reassess their strategies and tactics. This introspection can lead to personal growth and enhanced strategic planning.

Experiencing such potent fear can act as a wake-up call, encouraging them to improve their defences and prepare better for confrontations. It can serve as a catalyst for developing resilience and fortitude, making them more formidable opponents in the future.

The enchantment to make your enemies silent with fear is a powerful tool for seizing control and neutralizing opposition. It carries the dual advantage of controlling the narrative and discouraging offensive actions, benefiting both you and, in an unconventional way, your adversaries.

Ditau, Ridas, Atrosis, Uusur, Hispen, Histanos, Benatir

Ditau: DEE-tau
Ridas: REE-das
Atrosis: ah-TROH-sis
Uusur: OO-soor
Hispen: HIS-pen
Histanos: his-TAH-nos
Benatir: beh-NAH-teer

Enchant your enemies to reveal their plans

The depths of this profound power are designed to unravel the veiled intentions and concealed schemes of your adversaries. By invoking this enchantment, you gain the ability to compel your enemies to disclose their hidden plans, providing you with invaluable insight and a strategic advantage in navigating challenging circumstances.

The power allows you to pierce through the darkness of uncertainty and gain a glimpse into the intentions and actions of those who seek to oppose you. By uncovering their hidden strategies, you can strategically position yourself, counter their moves, and protect your interests effectively.

The advantages of this power extend beyond mere knowledge. By compelling your enemies to reveal their plans, you create an opportunity for pre-emptive action and effective defence. Armed with this newfound understanding, you can devise informed strategies, anticipate their moves, and mitigate potential risks. This power grants you the ability to stay one step ahead, empowering you to navigate conflicts with wisdom and finesse.

For your adversaries, although unintentional, revealing their plans can have a surprising benefit. Should their plans have been poorly conceived or detrimental, your counteractions could potentially save them from significant mistakes or losses.

The act of revealing their plans can lead them to question their strategies or intentions, possibly encouraging them to reassess their approach. This self-reflection can lead to more effective planning in the future.

Revealing their plans can prompt them to improve their defences or secrecy, making them harder to predict in the future. This adaptability can make them more formidable adversaries, pushing them to develop and grow.

The enchantment to make your enemies reveal their plans is a potent tool for gaining the upper hand in any conflict or competition. Its real power lies in its ability to provide strategic insight and expose vulnerabilities, benefiting both you and, indirectly, your adversaries.

In essence, this enchantment is not only about gaining strategic advantages but also about provoking self-reflection and adaptability. Causing an enemy to reflect, to pause, to look within, is one of the greatest weapons we possess.

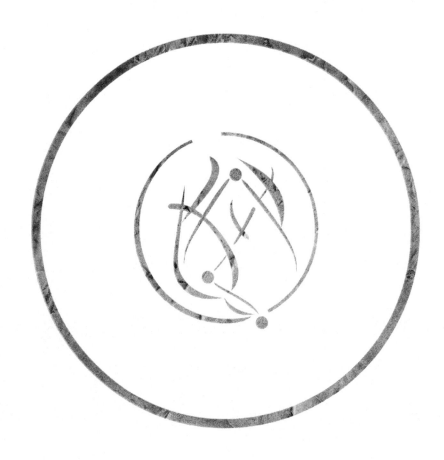

Raditus, Polastrien, Terpandu, Ostrata, Pericatur, Ermas

Raditus: rah-DEE-tus
Polastrien: poh-lah-STREE-en
Terpandu: ter-PAN-doo
Ostrata: ohs-TRAH-ta
Pericatur: peh-rih-KAH-tur
Ermas: ER-mas

Enchant a group to overcome a common obstacle

By invoking this power, you can inspire and empower a group to join forces, harmonize their efforts, and overcome a common obstacle that stands in their path.

The power holds immense potential for collective growth, resilience, and achievement. It allows you to harness the strength of unity, pooling together the unique talents, perspectives, and strengths of individuals towards a common goal. By rallying the group's collective energy, you foster a sense of camaraderie, collaboration, and unwavering determination.

When a group faces a shared obstacle, this enchantment serves as a catalyst for cohesion and progress. It ignites a sense of purpose, inspiring individuals to set aside personal differences and work harmoniously towards a shared vision. The power of collective action enables the group to tap into their combined resources, creativity, and resilience, resulting in a heightened likelihood of success.

This enchantment can have a transformative impact, not only for you but also for the group involved, providing a way forward amidst adversity.

For the group, the benefits of this enchantment are considerable. Overcoming a common obstacle strengthens the group's unity and resilience. Shared struggles and collective victories can create a strong bond, fostering a sense of community and shared accomplishment.

Surmounting a challenge often leads to growth. By navigating through the obstacle, the group can acquire new skills, knowledge, or perspectives. This collective learning can enhance the group's capabilities and readiness for future challenges.

Overcoming a common obstacle can create momentum for the group. The sense of achievement that comes from successfully navigating a challenge can energize the collective, inspiring them to take on further initiatives and maintain progress.

The enchantment to guide a group to overcome a common obstacle is a formidable tool for collective empowerment and can be used in combination with leadership for extremely rewarding results.

Saritap, Pernisox, Ottarim

Saritap: sah-REE-tap
Pernisox: per-nee-SOKS
Ottarim: oht-TAH-rim

Enchant a person to respect you

By harnessing this power, you can influence an individual to hold you in high regard. The effects of this enchantment can be far-reaching, creating a more supportive and rewarding dynamic between you and the enchanted individual. Respect can also be exploited to foster subservience, should that be required.

When someone respects you, they are more likely to value your opinion and consider your advice. This can prove particularly advantageous in discussions or decisions, enabling you to influence the outcome to better align with your preferences or interests.

Furthermore, respect often comes hand in hand with trust. By cultivating respect, you are likely also building a foundation of trust with the individual. This trust can facilitate smoother interactions and could open doors to opportunities that might only present themselves in the presence of mutual trust. Whether or not the trust is rewarded with honesty on your part is immaterial.

Gaining respect from another can greatly boost your confidence. It's an affirmation of your worth and capabilities, which can empower you to take on new challenges or pursue your ambitions with more conviction.

For the person who has been enchanted to respect you, this transformation can offer various advantages. Respect can be the cornerstone of healthy relationships. By respecting you, they are likely to engage in more positive interactions, leading to a more fruitful relationship that can enrich their personal or professional life.

The experience of respect often requires understanding and empathy. By learning to respect you, they may also develop these qualities, which can improve their interactions with others and contribute to their personal growth.

Respecting you might expose them to your experiences, knowledge, or perspectives that they may not have otherwise considered. This expanded view can broaden their horizons, stimulate their thinking, and potentially spark inspiration.

The enchantment to make a person respect you can shift dynamics and open doors. It's an enchantment that transforms dynamics, turning indifference or disdain into respect and understanding.

Nizael, Estarnas, Tantarez

Nizael: nee-ZAYL
Estarnas: eh-STAR-nas
Tantarez: tan-TA-rez

Enchant a group to welcome your ideas

You can inspire a group to wholeheartedly welcome your ideas, fostering an atmosphere of openness, receptiveness, and collaboration. This atmosphere may be illusory, but it is, nevertheless, effective.

You can influence a group to readily accept and welcome your ideas, even if they were previously indifferent or actively hostile. This can serve as a crucial instrument for manifesting your vision and can have an impact in various contexts, from personal gatherings to professional environments.

The most obvious benefit is that you will get your way, and others will have to stand aside. This may be all I need to say of this power but is worth exploring more subtle. applications.

The group's acceptance can elevate your position within that group. It's not just about gaining respect or admiration, but also about gaining influence. As your ideas are welcomed, you naturally assume a position of authority or leadership within the group, consolidating your position and enhancing your ability to steer the group's course.

The group also stands to gain from this enchantment. Being open to your ideas can stimulate intellectual growth within the group. Different perspectives encourage critical thinking and a more comprehensive understanding of issues at hand.

The welcoming of new ideas can stimulate creativity within the group. It's often through the exploration of different ideas that unique and innovative solutions are discovered. This could lead to breakthroughs and advancements that may otherwise have been overlooked.

The acceptance of your ideas can foster unity within the group. Shared ideas and common goals can bring people together, enhancing cooperation and fostering a sense of community. This can lead to more harmonious interactions and greater collective achievement.

The enchantment to make a group welcome your ideas is a powerful tool for personal advancement and collective progress. When a group of people believe in you, it becomes easier and easier to get what you need from them, without conflict or complication.

In its milder executions, this enchantment is a bridge of understanding, turning diversity of thought into collective strength, fostering creativity, and fostering unity within the group. At the more extreme end of the spectrum, it can make a roomful of fools see that you are, after all, the one that's right.

Senapos, Terfita, Estamos, Perfiter, Notarin

Senapos: seh-NAH-pos
Terfita: ter-FEE-ta
Estamos: es-TAH-mos
Perfiter: per-FEE-ter
Notarin: noh-TA-rin

Enchant a person to be open-minded

Designed to inspire an individual to embrace open-mindedness, you can create an atmosphere where someone becomes receptive to new ideas, perspectives, and experiences, fostering personal growth, expanded horizons, and effective communication.

The power holds immense potential for promoting understanding, fostering empathy, and nurturing harmonious relationships. It allows you to encourage someone to step beyond the boundaries of their preconceived notions, biases, and limitations, creating space for mutual respect, collaboration, and the exchange of diverse viewpoints.

You may also use the power to make somebody so open-minded that they become easily gullible in the presence of you and your ideas, to the point where it may be said that they are suggestible.

An immediate advantage of this power can be the facilitation of effective communication. An open-minded individual is more likely to consider your ideas and opinions, enabling constructive dialogue and reducing conflict. This can greatly enhance your interpersonal interactions, fostering harmony and mutual understanding. Do not assume you must always control others. In some circumstances, your greatest gain me be from an open connection, and all you need is to use this enchantment to make the other person as open as you are.

By encouraging open-mindedness in others, you indirectly create a more receptive audience for your thoughts and initiatives. This can prove particularly advantageous in situations where you aim to lead, innovate, or introduce change. Essentially, your enchantment helps lay the groundwork for your ideas to be accepted and appreciated.

For the enchanted individual, the journey towards open-mindedness can unlock a wealth of benefits. By becoming open-minded, they allow themselves to learn and grow by considering diverse viewpoints and ideas. This can lead to personal growth, a more nuanced understanding of the world, and even inspire creative thinking.

Open-mindedness often fosters empathy and understanding. By being open to other perspectives, the enchanted individual may become more compassionate, understanding, and tolerant. This transformation can greatly improve their relationships and social interactions.

Open-mindedness can lead to greater adaptability. An open-minded person is generally more comfortable with change and uncertainty, and they are better equipped to adapt to new situations or challenges. This trait can make them more resilient and successful in their personal and professional life.

This enchantment can be the seed of understanding and acceptance or a tool for influence, and I regard this as one of the finest powers I have ever used.

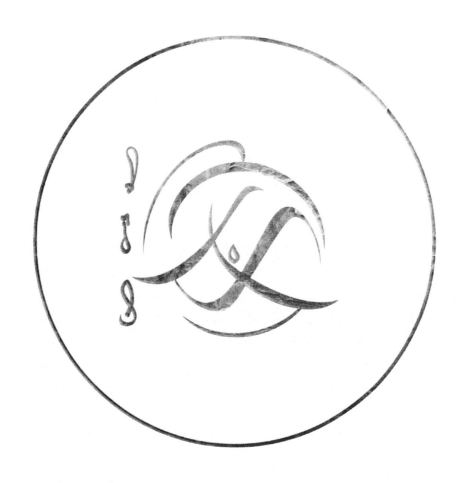

Turan, Estonos, Fuza, Vazotas, Testanar

Turan: too-RAN
Estonos: es-TOH-nos
Fuza: FOO-zah
Vazotas: vah-ZOH-tas
Testanar: tes-TAH-nar

Enchant a person to move away from their home

By calling upon this power, you can influence an individual to leave their current abode. This enchantment can prove highly beneficial in myriad ways. It could help you alleviate a tense neighbourly situation or create space for new dynamics in a shared living situation. Your living environment heavily influences your well-being, and this power offers a means to shape it according to your needs or desires.

Moreover, using this power could free up opportunities for you. Perhaps the person you wish to move is occupying a place of interest, or their departure could lead to opportunities that would otherwise not present themselves. In these instances, you could use this enchantment to align the circumstances in your favour.

In simple cases, you may have a neighbour who is noisy, or otherwise offensive, and disposing of them in this way is deeply satisfying.

For the one who becomes enchanted to move away from their home, this change can also bring about various benefits. Moving to a new place often signifies a fresh start. This could offer them the opportunity to break old patterns, explore new environments, and foster novel relationships, potentially enriching their life.

The change in scenery might stimulate personal growth. Adapting to a new environment often necessitates flexibility and resilience. The experience could therefore enhance these traits in the individual, better equipping them to handle future challenges.

The process of moving often incites introspection, encouraging individuals to reassess their belongings and life choices. It could prompt them to declutter not just their physical possessions, but also their mental and emotional baggage, leading to an overall improvement in their well-being.

You can direct the ritual simultaneously at several people if all are in the same vicinity. Otherwise, direct this magick at the key decision maker.

The enchantment to make a person move away from their home is a powerful tool to manipulate living dynamics. It is particularly potent in situations where the current living situation is in discord with your desires or well-being.

Reterrem, Salibat, Cratares, Hisater

Reterrem: reh-TER-rem
Salibat: sah-LEE-bat
Cratares: KRAH-tah-rez
Hisater: HEE-sah-ter

Enchant a person to become more disciplined

With this power, you can manipulate another person's mindset, fostering a strong inclination to adhere to rules, routines, and self-control, ultimately serving your personal goals and ambitions.

The power offers you the opportunity to exert influence over *their* willpower, moulding them into a more focused, determined, and self-disciplined individual who will adhere to your directives. If this person works for you or with you, the advantages are plain to see.

This power increases their efficiency and productivity, which can benefit you, especially if you are reliant on this person's actions for your personal or professional progress.

Their increased discipline can lead to better self-management, possibly resulting in positive changes such as improved health, better financial management, or an enhanced ability to cope with stress. Their personal growth could positively affect your relationship with them, leading to more harmonious interactions and mutual respect.

In a less generous mood, I might add that if you are burned by an undisciplined slob, somewhere in your life, this is a way to kick them back into order.

For the person who is enchanted to become more disciplined, they stand to gain a wealth of benefits. The newfound discipline can improve their overall quality of life, enabling them to achieve their goals more efficiently. It could lead to increased self-esteem and personal satisfaction, as they realize their potential to accomplish tasks they once found daunting.

Discipline often begets success. As the enchanted person begins to excel in their pursuits thanks to their heightened discipline, they may find doors of opportunity opening for them. Whether it's in their personal life, career, or hobbies, their success can lead to an enriched, fulfilled life.

Their journey towards becoming more disciplined can provide them with valuable life skills. The virtues of persistence, patience, and consistency that come hand in hand with discipline are not only beneficial in the present moment, but they are also tools that will serve them throughout their lives.

The potency of this enchantment can be harnessed in any situation that calls for improved discipline and self-management.

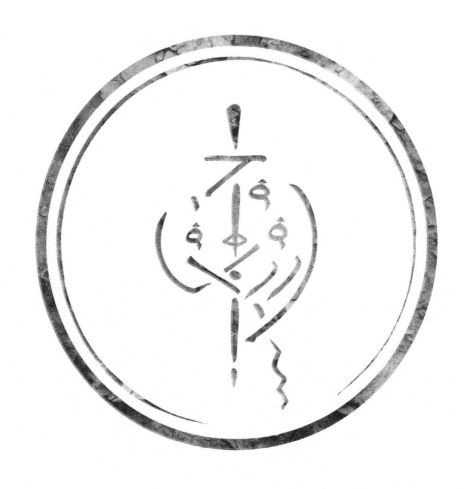

Crostes, Furinot, Katipa, Garinos

Crostes: KROHS-tes
Furinot: fyoo-REE-not
Katipa: kah-TEE-pah
Garinos: gah-REE-nos

Enchant your enemies to see your point of view

When you summon this power, you are able to turn the tide of opposition by aligning your enemies with your perspective. This enchantment has the potential to transform even the most fervent adversary into an unexpected ally, which in turn could fundamentally alter the dynamics of your personal or professional conflicts.

This alignment can serve to mitigate hostility, reduce resistance, and possibly even turn opposition into support for your cause or stance.

Having your enemies see your point of view broadens your influence, enabling you to wield a greater degree of control over situations and outcomes. This allows you to navigate challenging circumstances with enhanced dexterity and assurance, effectively shifting the odds in your favour.

For your adversaries, being enchanted to understand your perspective can prove to be an enlightening experience. It provides them with a fresh viewpoint, broadening their horizons and possibly instigating a revaluation of their own stance. This process could potentially trigger cognitive growth, allowing them to develop a more nuanced and comprehensive understanding of the situation at hand.

Seeing your point of view can serve to reduce their aggression and hostility. As they begin to empathize with your perspective, it can lead to more peaceful and constructive interactions. This transformation can create an opportunity for better conflict resolution, potentially leading to harmonious outcomes that are beneficial for all parties involved.

Through the enchantment, your enemies could discover a newfound respect for you, as understanding often breeds empathy and, subsequently, respect. As a result, the interpersonal dynamics can shift, replacing animosity with mutual understanding and possibly even cooperation.

Whether it's a minor disagreement or a major feud, this power can be employed to steer the situation towards a more favourable and harmonious outcome. While it can be used as beacon of understanding and transformation, capable of turning foes into friends and opposition into alignment, it can also be an excellent form of control and influence.

Osthariman, Visantiparos, Noctatur

Osthariman: ohs-tha-REE-man
Visantiparos: vee-SAN-tee-PAH-ros
Noctatur: NOK-ta-tur

Enchant another to stop legal action against you

Cast influence over the one seeking to bring legal action against you, and you will be protected from their intentions. This enchantment can bring a welcome respite from the burdens of legal stress, giving you the freedom to focus on other aspects of your life. It serves as an invaluable tool for self-preservation, potentially saving you from the numerous detriments of legal action - financial loss, reputation damage, and emotional distress.

This power enables you to exert control over the situation, and for all people of significance, control is the cornerstone of progress. Legal proceedings can often feel unpredictable and daunting. By enchanting another to cease legal action, you reclaim the reins, determining the course of events according to your desires.

You may even use this once a legal action is well-underway. If tomorrow is you first day in court, you still have time to put this to use. It may not be as effective when used so late in the day, but it is certainly worth trying.

The power can also serve to redefine your relationship with the individual who intends to take legal action. By altering their intent, you create an opportunity to mend fences, possibly turning an adversary into an ally. In other cases, you may crush their will to compete with you in any manner.

To frame this in a way that benefits the individual you enchant, know that the individual can also benefit. Legal proceedings can be lengthy, stressful, and costly for both parties involved. By ceasing legal action, they free themselves from these burdens, affording them peace of mind and financial savings.

The act of forgiving or seeking non-legal means to resolve the dispute can lead to personal growth. It can encourage them to practice empathy, forgiveness, and open-mindedness - traits that can enhance their personal relationships and overall quality of life.

Opting to discontinue legal action may also allow them to maintain or restore their relationship with you. Instead of locking horns in a legal battle, they can choose to negotiate, compromise, or reconcile, thus preserving social or professional ties. Whether this is a true potential, or only one they perceive, has no bearing on the effect of the magick.

The power to enchant another to stop legal action against you is a potent tool, especially valuable when confronted with serious charges or litigious individuals.

While it promotes resolution over conflict, persuasion over coercion, and harmony over discord, it also enables more covert victories to take place.

Hocatos, Imorad, Surater, Trumantrem, Ricona

Hocatos: hoh-KAH-tos
Imorad: ee-MOH-rad
Surater: soo-RAH-ter
Trumantrem: troo-MAN-trem
Ricona: ree-KOH-nah

Enchant a group to fight on your behalf

When you call upon this power, you assemble a metaphorical army willing to stand up for you, even in the face of great adversity. This enchantment forges a legion of loyalty, ready to defend your interests, giving you a formidable sense of security and protection. Beyond mere physical defence, this group can also fight your battles in various realms - social, political, or even psychological, reinforcing your stance and amplifying your voice against opposition.

Additionally, commanding a group that is prepared to fight for you can enhance your influence and reputation. As they rally behind your cause, your prominence and authority are bolstered, making your words and actions reverberate more powerfully within your community. Their unwavering support can provide emotional strength in challenging situations, reinforcing your resolve and boosting your confidence.

The very act of being supported in battle can be empowering. The assurance of not standing alone but having a team ready to fight for you can instil a sense of invincibility, encouraging you to dare more and fear less.

From the standpoint of the enchanted group, being part of your legion brings a sense of purpose and camaraderie. Their collective action in your defence fosters a feeling of unity, promoting strong bonds within the group. Their involvement in your battles may provide them with a platform for self-expression, a chance to voice their views, and stand up for what they believe in. It can also offer them a sense of empowerment, being part of a group that has the power to effect change.

Standing up for your cause can also result in personal growth for the group members. As they face the trials and tribulations of your battles, they may find their courage, resilience, and strategic skills tested and honed, leading to personal development and growth.

In essence, this enchantment establishes a dynamic symbiosis between you and the enchanted group, creating an alliance that thrives on lapparent oyalty, unity, and mutual empowerment.

Nista, Saper, Visnos, Xatros, Nifer, Roxas, Rortos

Nista: NEE-sta
Saper: SAY-per
Visnos: VEEZ-nos
Xatros: ZAH-tros
Nifer: NEE-fer
Roxas: ROX-as
Rortos: ROHR-tos

Enchant a person to trust you with money

When someone trusts you with their money, it opens doors to new financial opportunities. Their willingness to invest, lend, or provide financial resources can fuel your ventures, expand your business prospects, and accelerate your financial growth.

By calling forth this power, you weave a web of financial trust around the person enchanted. Such an enchantment could potentially open doors to financial opportunities that might have been previously unattainable, fuelling your ambitions, be they personal, professional, or otherwise.

Being trusted with money can elevate your social standing and reputation, as financial trust often signifies trust in character and ability, leading to increased respect and influence among peers.

Another facet of this power lies in the way it alters your relationship with the enchanted. Entrusted with their financial matters, you become more deeply entwined in their life, leading to a closer, more significant connection. This connection could reveal new facets of their personality, or even open new avenues for interaction and engagement.

The act of being trusted with money can in itself be empowering. The confidence that the enchanted person shows in your ability to manage financial matters can instil in you a sense of accomplishment and competence, which can further enhance your self-esteem.

The person who trusts you with their money also benefits. They gain the comfort of knowing their financial matters are in safe hands, which can bring a sense of peace and security. It can also free them from the stresses and burdens of managing their finances, allowing them more time and energy to devote to other aspects of life.

Entrusting you with their money could potentially lead to financial growth for them, as you might be able to manage or invest their funds better.

The act of entrusting someone with money can be an empowering experience for them. It can signify a shift in their perspective towards money and trust, opening up their minds to new possibilities and ways of relating to others.

The enchantment to make a person trust you with money is a powerful tool that, when wielded properly, can lead to significant shifts in relationships, status, and financial conditions. Its potency can be tapped into regardless of the amount of money in question.

This enchantment can form a bond of mutual benefit between you and the enchanted, or it can allow you to dance on the thrilling edge of financial adventure.

Rokes, Pilatus, Zotas, Tulitas, Xatanitos

Rokes: ROH-kes
Pilatus: pee-LAH-tus
Zotas: ZOH-tas
Tulitas: too-LEE-tas
Xatanitos: zah-tah-NEE-tos

Enchant a person to give up bad habits effortlessly

Engaging this power allows you to influence a person's behaviour so profoundly that they can break away from undesirable habits without exerting strenuous effort. This enchantment possesses the potential to accelerate personal growth, foster healthier lifestyles, and enable significant behavioural transformation.

You have the ability to guide and influence the evolution of a person's character and lifestyle. Watching someone transform, largely due to your influence, can be a gratifying experience.

Fostering healthier habits in a person can enhance your relationship with them. As they attribute their positive changes to your influence, their respect and affection for you may grow. In many instances, the strengthened bond could create an ally or a dependable friend, offering you emotional support and companionship.

Having a person adopt better habits can result in direct benefits for you, especially if they were directly annoying. For example, if you live with someone who repeatedly performs an action - any action - that you find infuriating, the peace and relief can be tremendous, when that habit is eliminated.

For the person influenced to give up bad habits, the benefits are substantial and transformative. Breaking away from those habits can significantly improve their physical health and mental well-being. The transition to a healthier lifestyle, for example, could lead to increased vitality, enhanced mood, and improved quality of life.

As they overcome their habits, they gain a sense of achievement and self-efficacy. This can boost self-esteem and self-confidence, which in turn, promotes personal growth and resilience.

The eradication of bad habits can open up new opportunities for them. Free from the constraints of unhealthy habits, they have more time and energy to explore new interests, pursue personal goals, and engage in more fulfilling activities.

The process of effortlessly giving up bad habits can serve as a life lesson, making them realise the potential for change within themselves. This can inspire them to continuously strive for self-improvement and personal growth, further enhancing their life journey.

This is an enchantment that promotes wellness, growth, and resilience, and it can be created as a gift. Or it can be more covert, used to bring peace to your life.

Actatos, Catipta, Bejouran, Itapan, Marnutus

Actatos: ahk-TAH-tos
Catipta: kah-TEEP-ta
Bejouran: beh-joo-RAN
Itapan: ee-TAH-pan
Marnutus: mar-NOO-tus

Enchant a person to give you valuable guidance

Summoning this extraordinary power, the enchanter sets in motion a chain of events that leads to the acquisition of a resourceful advisor in the person they enchant. This individual becomes a precious asset, a guiding light in navigating life's twists and turns. The wisdom they offer can be a catalyst for your success, providing a clearer vision to your ambitions and propelling you towards your goals.

But the benefits extend beyond mere guidance. The person enchanted becomes a trusted sounding board, offering fresh perspectives and ideas that stimulate your creativity and sharpen your problem-solving skills. Their input creates a harmonious exchange of thoughts, nurturing a rich and vibrant intellectual landscape.

The beauty of this enchantment lies not only in the guidance received but also in the deep interpersonal connection it fosters. As you regularly seek and receive their advice, the bond between you and the enchanted person grows stronger. Trust and mutual understanding intertwine, forging a profound connection that transcends the realm of typical relationships. It is within this sacred space that vulnerability thrives, allowing you to explore the depths of your aspirations and fears, guided by their unwavering support.

On the other side of the enchantment, the person enchanted assumes the role of an esteemed advisor, a beacon of knowledge that radiates with purpose. Being entrusted with the weight of your dreams and aspirations brings a profound sense of self-worth and validation. Their advice serves as a testament to their value in your life, highlighting their unique perspective and profound insights.

The act of providing guidance becomes a transformative experience for them as well. With each interaction, their own cognitive abilities flourish, nurturing their wisdom and understanding of the world.

Engaging in this enchantment infuses purpose and meaning into both lives. For the enchanter, it offers new insights and perspectives in every situation, no matter the gravity. But its true potency shines through during significant decision-making or critical crossroads. In these pivotal moments, the enchantment becomes a beacon of clarity, illuminating the path forward.

Together, the enchanter and the enchanted forge an extraordinary alliance. The enchantment forms a gateway to wisdom and success, cultivating a unique synergy that transcends the boundaries of typical relationships. Through this profound connection, both parties thrive, their lives intertwined in a tapestry of shared experiences and growth.

Ritas, Onalun, Tersorit, Serpitas, Quitathar, Zamarath

Ritas: REE-tas
Onalun: oh-NAH-loon
Tersorit: ter-SOH-rit
Serpitas: sur-PEE-tas
Quitathar: kwee-TAH-thar
Zamarath: zah-mah-RATH

Further Reading

#1 Occult Best-Sellers available from
The Power of Magick Publishing

7 Occult Money Rituals
by Henry Archer

The Magick of Angels and Demons
by Henry Archer

Angelic Sigils, Seals and Calls
by Ben Woodcroft

Angelic Protection Magick
by Ben Woodcroft

The Angel Overlords
By Ben Woodcroft

Angelic Trance Magick
by Ben Woodcroft

The Power of Magick Publishing

www.thepowerofmagick.com

Made in United States
North Haven, CT
12 June 2023

37652622R00065